Free Verse Editions
Edited by Jon Thompson

What People Are Saying about *Go On*

Go On directs us to notice and to know the world with perfect vulnerability. The delights and difficulties trickling through the chinks of ordinary time swirl through these deceptively simple verses that, like Blake's, hum with the certainty of divine presence always near us but nearly always beyond comprehension. Rackin's expert development of the lyric's oldest properties carries forth the unpredictable relationship between human awareness and the visible world through "elemental shifts" of spare, simple words that glimpse the unseen and touch its consciousness. "It's not supposed to make sense," these graceful poems inform us, but our responsibility lies in baring ourselves emotionally and intellectually to others and the world as we make and find it. Only in this state of exposure, "shirt open/ chest full of birds," do we gather the often fleeting, sometimes lasting rewards of hope and faith.

—*Elizabeth Savage*

Go On

Ethel Rackin

Parlor Press
Anderson, South Carolina
www.parlorpress.com

Parlor Press LLC, Anderson, South Carolina, 29621

© 2017 by Parlor Press
All rights reserved.
Printed in the United States of America
S A N: 2 5 4 - 8 8 7 9

Library of Congress Cataloging-in-Publication Data

Names: Rackin, Ethel, author.
Title: Go on / Ethel Rackin.
Description: Anderson, South Carolina : Parlor Press, [2017] |
Series: Free Verse Editions
Identifiers: LCCN 2016047083 (print) | LCCN 2016055957
(ebook) | ISBN 9781602357969 (softcover : acid-free paper) |
ISBN 9781602357976 (pdf) | ISBN 9781602357983 (epub)
| ISBN 9781602357990 (ibook) | ISBN 9781602358003
(mobi)
Classification: LCC PS3618.A343 A6 2017 (print) | LCC
PS3618.A343 (ebook) | DDC 811/.6--dc23
LC record available at https://lccn.loc.gov/2016047083

2 3 4 5

Cover design by David Blakesley.
Cover image: Rebecca Hoenig. "Grandma's Game." 1998. Mixed
media. Used by permission.
Printed on acid-free paper.
Parlor Press, LLC is an independent publisher of scholarly and
trade titles in print and multimedia formats. This book is available
in paperback and ebook formats from Parlor Press on the World
Wide Web at http://www.parlorpress.com or through online and
brick-and-mortar bookstores. For submission information or to
find out about Parlor Press publications, write to Parlor Press,
3015 Brackenberry Drive, Anderson, South Carolina, 29621, or
email editor@parlorpress.com.

For Phyllis and Donald Rackin

Contents

Contents

Go On

Time does go on—
I tell it gay to those who suffer now—
They shall survive—
There is a sun—
They don't believe it now—

—Emily Dickinson, 1121

If Ida goes on, does she go on even when she does not
go on any more. No and Yes.

—Gertrude Stein, Ida

Go On

You've slept in the sun too long
the musician you seek
carrying a sheet of notes
under the cypress tree
is in no way more real
than you are now
his are sideways looks
that take too long
meanwhile the shoals
that marshal evening
will soon arrive
and of them you speak
but have nothing really to say
stay in the park a little longer reading
go down to the water if you like
the emptiness you seek also takes time.

Night Boats

The night-drifting boats that glide across the sea
are particular about it—this is their Atlantic
and they are definitely approaching something
how then can I be distressed
for they have taken on the work
my life has demanded
they have taken and given back
while I am solitary—one of billions—
besides the stars will soon shine down
the sea recede briefly to return again.

To the New Year

Those are woods I would have chosen
the fright or fight I would have favored
for favors like this—
like the wooden forms of fauns—
come with tags
and glue like this will last
only as long—
meanwhile night is supple
its surpluses surprising
while the lost are lost
for a very long time
and the face of recognition
is the face of longing that lasts.

Cascais

These lovers under the catalpa trees
beside the peacock—its aqua neck
its green tan orange and gold feathers—
one sighs the other laughs
the laughter of teenagers
and it is you now who chases
the peacock for its picture
trying not to stare
after centuries of loss
in the last century.

Largesse

In attending the largest wood
whoever thought of falling fell
the last word in a fairy's trees
the thought that would fall
in a largely berry-covered wood
the attention of falling
in a woolen wood
wrapt and largely falling—
a feller's tree—
the largest wood—or word—
largely covered in berries
now buried in a family tree.

Soledad

The anger you feel is real
the birds can attest to it
for there they swerve—
trying to relinquish something—
not that they care one bit
about your grief—
its exact contours
its secret recesses—
meanwhile one in particular
rehearses the show.

In an Ancient Forest

Betwixt a grove of trees—
flowers, fir, and ferns—
in the drunken forest I
have seen it—
with mine own eyes—
true for a girl on this side.

Your Kind

Seals trees and sends bark back to the ship
a slip of paper has made it through
to you it is only a slip—
but paper is for birds
who know how to put it in pouches
and save for the day—

Mont Sainte-Victoire

The same subject seen from a different angle offers subject for
study of the most powerful interest and so varied that I think
I could occupy myself for months without changing place, by
turning now more to the right, now more to the left.

—*Paul Cézanne in a letter to his son, 1906*

A mountain fades
and is outlined
where light is
now part of it.

~

A picture of an arc
and the story
orange as paint
as earth
always the cut-off
the raised binoculars.

~

Coming into something
now that rocks and trees
singing trees
and elemental shifts
now story views
mounting a growing affection.

Etruscan Hills

Shadows over Etruscan hills
hills which are sad
those which still show
conquered by Romans in snow
shadows on Etruscan hills
on them and in them too
hills we see and iconic ones
existed in an era in which
they were sold and laid waste to
towers of hills—one or two shifting—
birds strung out along a line of ice
taken in or else sold.

Afflux

Like a seed—
the *coeur* in flower
the sweet remains of sour
the worriless hour
an anchorless tugboat
on the high seas
notches in trees
a keyhole for your keys
the pince-nez you need
the *S* in speed.

Bird So High

High as a bird can be
a draught through
an open window—
a drift of snow
a bird so high
high as it flew!

Villa

Villa-style tract houses
and tracks with horses

the career track
the tracks we left

coming on suddenly—
becoming life—

as if the before and after had frozen
and couldn't be tracked down.

Durée

A note came down on a wing
formed in apartment clusters
in the apartment clusters—war—
dimensions were lost directions
to the specified courtyard—
a door in the wall
opening to both—grey
emptying out and in.

House in Winter

It's not supposed to make sense—
a bird's wing—some lost thread—
a chill has come and with it
several semi-warm coats and
the cost of heat for a house this big—
a chill has come and into it
several need-blind birds fly.

Christmas Dance

That lovely dance
you thought
was yours
wrapped round
the tree
and stood
a jeweled throne
for those who'd go
for those who
stood above
the words
you wore
you thought
were yours—
a lonely dance
in tangled wood
unwrapped
the tree
there stood.

The Moth

Mercury rising—
heals bells—
lust's hollow hotels
silhouettes of smoke-
struck actresses—
stalactites silbilants—
fluid violent triumphs
of nymphs' fluted
violin marches
silicate staircases
silent sentences
while myrmidons fire
asunder—wonder—
fairy children
who are charmed
are haunted—
must add water
address winter
in the days to come
the moths months become.

Maternal

After Rebecca Hoenig's "Grandma's Game"

Forever may you flower
at the cost that it might matter
and the joy of garden powers
the zip of ovu pater
as maternal pets sew cookies
Miss Shulman's gold trousseau
joy to live in candy
and the craft of love's woe
the tub is filled too
and the toy pins are his.

Home Blessing

Bless this sheer force
of imagined wellbeing
dwelling has come
and into it an escape.

Bless this home living
and the escape of music
however far in the wall
of home being's blessed
the music will swell
and swell into it—mere!—
for the blessed music's mine
and the indwelling besides.

Bless this inhabitation
which takes delight
in lowest compartments—
struck or sunk
divine or dive
towering stage's triple-dance.

Bless this state
locked inside acrid apartments
finding a shingle to pick
remember the needle-hatch
to write—scars are fields—

Bless this mess and the streets.

American Fix

Dug the truck out of Phil's garage but didn't know where Phil had gone.

~

Enough love and song on the byways
enough coming to grips.

~

Before I could tell another's lie I was lying in it.

Bombs

Which stream—
like fortune cookie wrappers—
crush and bury—
continue to occupy—
highest towers—
glare from speakers.

Imperialisms

It isn't impressive—
the imperious start—
the anxious fix—
there's torture to it—
the getaway cars
and stolen libraries
are not irrelevant—
hidden as if some star
wouldn't look asunder—
and do we know it.

The Field

Let this luck come
let this looking back break
let the lost years
around the bend
encircle us
pick us up
let the years of loss
and the burdens bend
let lies be lost
like shadows that creep
across this field at night
looking for light
let those who'd hold us
come out of forest's bend
into cerulean green.

Vita Nuova

Surely you'll want to find a race
for the aloneness you're becoming
in writing this I can say for sure
you'll find your beginning
and finding the way love has
in coming—a fine beginning
you'll have again—
for a chance to find a new race
is in the air for beginners like you.

Unlikely Love Song

This exchange is not to be changed
this change is not to be exchanged
this logarithm is not to be lost
for whispered loss will surely last
in weather like this—in weather like this—
this temperamental bird sits on a leaf
this leaf is shaken in weather like this
this temperature gauge is gone these days
it's too hot to say—love—too hot to say
this drawer of salt's scrubbed
this dresser's mirror's smudged
this smudge of leaves and whispered chirps
are not to be changed—love—not to be changed.

Backlit

Rotten porches
money concealed in a box
the repeated *take a deep breath and exhale*
of someone in love
a building that topples over
flowers that flower or do not
and then you get this feeling of elevation—

My Life's Not Fancy

It's sweet and simple and old.

Recovered Dailies

12/5/05

And then there's Jean
across the street
tending to Bob
after his heart attack
and Jean's daughter and Kyle
driving the dark road to the hospital
because Jean can't see well
and I feel I could drown
inside this marriage.

6/5/06

Good time for a poem—
diecast evening
too many things to remember—
call Jean make plans for Friday
sad Eric's letter—return-to-sender.
Meanwhile roses drop dew.
Insides stand out more.
Those at an angle tilt
to stream and stretch
to ripen fail to rip
the page in half.
Baking's done.
Weekend's done too.
Arcades of thought
in which the church—
I'll have to write
about its spire or spine
another day.

6/25/06

Too black to really see the garden
though greens look greener
on account of so much rain.
Lilies tilt downward
for the weight of water
and pinks suddenly appear.
        Or is it just me visible
in the blackened trunks?
Meanwhile this feeling
on the street—
learn to imitate drama—
shirt open
chest full of birds
for no other reason
than you are here.

6/30/06

For a few days the street was closed
due to flooding.

Still and all you did not come
to the churchyard.
Seeing war seeds grow up
watching the trumpet
flowers turn and fall to the ground.

This too becomes tiresome—
the statue stands perennially—
     notice me
observe my way toward sun.

Sun shines and ducks
behind clouds.
It lifts these girls
who speak so much
surprising the presence
of choppers!

Flood's crest,
the long hook around
on the toll-bridge home.

7/5/06

If the rain makes everything wet—
Dry it.
New flowers will spring up or be planted.
Tiny dots of color stay in the picture.
Grass is green and soft also.
The stone cairn behind the virgin
reminds me of a night we played outside.
We acted as if getting caught was tantamount
to dying.

[undated]

R.G. Simpson Electric Co.
Residential Commercial
parked in front of the churchyard
this morning everything's different.

You have to line it up with water and then where are you?

The flowers are happy in partial sun
it's not too hot yet at 9:30
as I sit here separated by glass
a butterfly circles.

Weekend Wedding [undated]

A mugginess sticks to trees
while the church looks frozen
inside must be a wedding
a white limousine sits right
of center as man and woman enter
fumes from cars affect leaves
and blooms of the churchyard.
Connie says traffic noise makes birds
chirp louder. Motorcycles loudest.

Ruins [undated]

At night when I'm wishing
the stars would fall through the glass
and steal kisses.

Interior View of Trees

Looking out at those pines—
the row that looms in the study window
the ones that run along the companion side
to the ruts of the gutter which stretch in a channel
to carry rain water away from the house
and often fail—due to a chink in the row
due to some defect—remember
the trees so bright when you're gone
the effort it took to live here.

Janus

The shadows we've come to know
burden us—
as though the frosting was the cake
we bite into it as widows do—
as werewolves—trespassers
we are respectful
knowing full well this land is your land.

Lux

In the solitary space of days
I have come to this hospital
of aliveness
and it is this I wish to secure
this I wish to occupy
for animals of aloneness
also seek refuge—only
the pinks of them emerge.

Money Tree

When you're in your house
with your lost contacts
your secret drawer
your fellow feeling fading
the thing for opening
those others hurting
their numbers dwindling
your own debt tree growing
the things you're discarding—
clothing, dishes, garbage—
all the while knowing—
what lies beneath the counter—
forgetting.

My Bare Acquisition

All I want of the things
is for them to be for me—
hidden—real—shiny—
sometimes stupid things
not for some others—
especially not for a great
number of others—
nor do I wish them
to have a different fate—
it is all of them I wish
to get the raw thing—
how real of my brain
to want them shiny
how seemingly sweet.

North Branch, Ferndale, Highbranch

The luck you make
is the luck you find—
this found luck
will carry you—
a seam in season
it finds lost birds
dirty in stations—
this big found bird
on the scene
is also a kind of luck—
it follows you
to the same north branch.

Advice

Dear Ones,
wait 'til sixty and turn.

~

Hyper-fix-it.

~

It's everybody's business
the way the tailor sews it.

~

You can't be loose and play
when your teeth are being ripped out
by dreams.

~

Folksingers will come to you
but not now
not anytime soon.

~

The grief you imagine
is easier than the grief you actually
have to live through.

~

All ways.

Sailors & Saints

Lay me down sailors
lay me down saints
I've passed the time longing
for what a ring is worth
these roads are long
and headed north
the languorous time
of wreaths for whatever
they're worth.

The Route

I was down on a route—
the trees there were trees
and many more like them
the question as to whether they were real trees
whether they were standing in for something else
whether you could mill their sap or what
honestly honestly never came up
there was a row of them
along the route
the route I said I was on—
and am—down by the river.

Sin Tiempo

Sometimes the thread is lost
as a tariff grows
triumphantly engaged
entrenched with longing
encircling the wearer—
wanderer—
and weather grows higher
or disturbance is ineluctably
drawn on undertone's tongue
on this list's tired listener
while for tomorrow's sake
notwithstanding each other
each anchor turns—is twisted—
into a kind of knot—heart.

Streaming

Too much time
on the line
and too much pining—
screens shine bright
the same bare longing
lingering—
and too much time
pining for crossings
signs the blighted mind
glares out of pine
or whiter skies
crowd the clouds
no brighter than their linings.

Tune

That's not a tune I know
that's an old show tune
or an out of tune show—
the kind I'd show you
if you were still here
eating strawberries
in the back room—
if you only knew.

The Hole

The hole you've dug is deep enough to see waves
and wide enough to see the foam that forms around edges.

~

Some of your old friends have started to call you names.

~

If I were you I'd stay there too for the forever you've created in it.

Poem

I kept wanting it only it was—
the jicama trees
the smell of slaw burning
what I found in my chest
was a desperate longing
for the lives of others
the sound of trees rattling
the monotonous so sweet of it all
talking or not talking
writing to keep it from happening
the channel set to sunset
by this time the lives accumulated
in my human brain
live chatting with others.

Envoi

The search for new sensations
turns up the naked body of a woman
as rain darkens the trees
a newspaper is read and collected
the Korean president and the American one
both wearing dark glasses
the trunks of a tree and traces of the woman
turn up in a neighborhood lake—
nobody is suspected
but the course of love is rerouted
however circuitous the route may be
the time-sensitive nature of flowers—
nature rains over them pummeling them
and they lose their stamens pistils stems petals
and leaves—the clatter in the dark house
where passages in a Gothic novel grow heavy
with the scent of lilac—the first right of spring.

Orange Tree

Let the orange tree grow
let it find its breeze
let its latter parts lag
its earlier parts too
let this leader learn
not to shine too brightly
lest it finds it grows
like a ladder
a trellis-like vine
let this star live long
let it find its peace
let it—homeless
in a breeze—
come home.

There Are Flowers

And there is a well
beyond these mills.

Acknowledgments

Grateful acknowledgement is made to the following publications, in which poems from *Go On* first appeared, some in different form: *Colorado Review, Kestrel,* and *Yew.*

Thank you to Jon Thompson and David Blakesley for their generous attention. Thank you to my colleagues and friends for their support, including Anna Badkhen, Christopher Bursk, Christophe Casamassima, Gillian Conoley, Stephen N. doCarmo, Kasey Jueds, Joanne Leva, Randall Potts, Donald Revell, James Richardson, Hassen Saker, Elizabeth Savage, and Gerald Stern. Love and gratitude to Rebecca Hoenig, Phyllis and Donald Rackin, and Dan Spirer.

About the Author

Ethel Rackin is the author of a previous collection of poems, *The Forever Notes*, published by Parlor Press in 2013. Her poems, book reviews, and collaborations have appeared in journals such as *Colorado Review, Hotel Amerika, Jacket2, Kenyon Review, Verse Daily*, and *Volt*. She earned her MFA from Bard College and her PhD in English Literature from Princeton University. She is currently an associate professor at Bucks County Community College in Pennsylvania.

Photograph of the author by Julie Schoettle. Used by permission.

Free Verse Editions

Edited by Jon Thompson

13 ways of happily by Emily Carr
Between the Twilight and the Sky by Jennie Neighbors
Blood Orbits by Ger Killeen
The Bodies by Chris Sindt
The Book of Isaac by Aidan Semmens
Canticle of the Night Path by Jennifer Atkinson
Child in the Road by Cindy Savett
Condominium of the Flesh by Valerio Magrelli, trans. by Clarissa Botsford
Contrapuntal by Christopher Kondrich
Country Album by James Capozzi
The Curiosities by Brittany Perham
Current by Lisa Fishman
Dismantling the Angel by Eric Pankey
Divination Machine by F. Daniel Rzicznek
Erros by Morgan Lucas Schuldt
Fifteen Seconds without Sorrow by Shim Bo-Seon, translated by Chung Eun-Gwi
   and Brother Anthony of Taizé
The Forever Notes by Ethel Rackin
The Flying House by Dawn-Michelle Baude
Go On by Ethel Rackin
Instances: Selected Poems by Jeongrye Choi, translated by Brenda Hillman,
   Wayne de Fremery, & Jeongrye Choi
The Magnetic Brackets by Jesús Losada, translated by Michael Smith &
   Luis Ingelmo
Man Praying by Donald Platt
A Map of Faring by Peter Riley
No Shape Bends the River So Long by Monica Berlin & Beth Marzoni
Overyellow, by Nicolas Pesquès, translated by Cole Swensen
Physis by Nicolas Pesque, translated by Cole Swensen
Pilgrimage Suites by Derek Gromadzki
Pilgrimly by Siobhán Scarry
Poems from above the Hill & Selected Work by Ashur Etwebi, translated by
   Brenda Hillman & Diallah Haidar
The Prison Poems by Miguel Hernández, translated by Michael Smith
Puppet Wardrobe by Daniel Tiffany
Quarry by Carolyn Guinzio
remanence by Boyer Rickel